DRAW WITH ME, DAD!

DRAW, COLOR, AND CONNECT WITH YOUR CHILD

Quarto is the authority on a wide range of topics.

Quarto educates, entertains and enriches the lives of our readers—enthusiasts and lovers of hands-on living.

www.quartoknows.com

First published in the United States of America in 2016 by
Race Point Publishing, a member of
Quarto Publishing Group USA Inc.
142 West 36th Street, 4th Floor
New York, New York 10018
www.quartoknows.com

10 9 8 7 6 5 4 3 2 1

ISBN 978-1-63106-199-8

Library of Congress Cataloging-in-Publication Data

Names: Narayan, Jasmine, author.
Title: Draw with me, dad! : draw, color, and connect with your child /
   Jasmine Narayan ; illustrated by Chad Geran.
Description: New York : Race Point Publishing, 2016. | Series: A side-by-side
   book
Identifiers: LCCN 2015050360 | ISBN 9781631061998 (paperback)
Subjects: LCSH: Parenting. | Father and child. | Coloring books. |
   Art--Social aspects. | Child development. | BISAC: JUVENILE NONFICTION /
   Art / Drawing. | JUVENILE NONFICTION / Concepts / Colors. | JUVENILE
   NONFICTION / Family / General (see also headings under Social Issues).
Classification: LCC HQ755.8 .N3573 2016 | DDC 306.874/2--dc23 LC record available at
http://lccn.loc.gov/2015050360

Editorial Director: Jeannine Dillon
Managing Editor: Erin Canning
Project Editor: Jason Chappell
Interior Design: Karla Baker
Cover Design: Tara Long

Printed in China

CONTENTS

4 INTRODUCTION BY JASMINE NARAYAN, PSY.D.

13 SELF-PERCEPTION
31 RELATIONSHIPS
49 HOME LIFE
67 SCHOOL LIFE
85 IMAGINATION
107 PLAY

126 REFERENCES
127 ABOUT THE AUTHOR
127 ABOUT THE ILLUSTRATOR

INTRODUCTION

A CHILD ASKS HIS DAD WHEN HE GETS HOME, "CAN I PLAY ON YOUR PHONE?"

"SURE," SAYS DAD HANDING OVER THE PHONE.

WHILE THE CHILD SETTLES INTO THE GAME, DAD ASKS, "SO HOW WAS SCHOOL TODAY?"

THE CHILD, BARELY LOOKING UP FROM THE PHONE ANSWERS, "MMM GOOD."

"WHAT DID YOU DO?" DAD ASKS, GENUINELY INTERESTED.

THE CHILD, NOW COMPLETELY ENGAGED IN THE GAME, DOES NOT RESPOND.

"COME ON, TELL ME WHAT YOU DID TODAY IN SCHOOL?"

"I DON'T KNOW. STUFF," THE CHILD MUMBLES.

DAD SIGHS.

Sound familiar? You have probably had such an interaction (or a similar one) with your child. All you want is just a little information about what his or her day was like, but getting him or her to open up thoughtfully is sometimes more difficult than pulling teeth!

As a dad, you are probably constantly handling the demands on your time: from helping out at home to your career to being a personal chauffer. One of the biggest complaints from parents today is about time—there is not enough time to do everything that you *need* to do, never mind all the things that you *want* to do.

With all those demands on your time, it can be difficult to find the time to slow down and authentically connect with your children even for 10 or 15 minutes. When I say authentically connect, I mean the "sit-down, look-them-in-the-eye, focus-on-them-and-only-them" kind of connection. And even if you can find 10 or 15 minutes a day to do this, how do you do it with a child who doesn't seem to want to connect or perhaps doesn't open up as readily as you'd like? Opportunities to interact like these do not always appear spontaneously, and nothing is more frustrating than giving your child your undivided attention, only to have him or her respond with vague answers.

WHY INTERROGATION DOESN'T WORK

Getting a child to open up about his or her day can be hard, particularly with the question-answer approach. Working with children in a therapeutic setting, I have experienced how asking even a well-intentioned question can backfire, especially if a child is reluctant to talk about a topic. Asking too many questions can cause a child to become distracted, respond with the dreaded "I don't know," or shut down completely (imagine shrugging shoulders or even fingers in ears).

Parents tend to rely on their children's verbal expression as a means to understand how they are spending their days, what they are learning in school, and the ways in which they interact with the outside world. Yet, children communicate in so many ways besides verbal language: they use their facial expressions; they use their actions and behaviors; and they love to use creative expression like drawing and coloring.

Their inner worlds are expansive and often defy the logic and reason of our adult world. It makes sense that to delve into your child's inner world you will have to use something other than just language.

Art activities have been used since the 1930s in child-centered play therapy as a means to help children feel comfortable, build trust, and facilitate the process of sharing feelings and thoughts. Drawing and coloring are especially effective tools! When a child's hands are busy and his or her focus is on a calm, repetitive activity, it is easier for a child's mind to feel free and at ease. Drawing and coloring with your child is a perfect recipe for open, spontaneous conversation and can give you a window into your child's internal world—it is a chance to engage in an authentic connection that might be hard to experience in other situations.

HOW TO USE THIS BOOK

Draw with Me, Dad! is called a "Side-by-Side Book" because it was created specifically to help you connect and encourage open conversation with your child all while enjoying the relaxing, peaceful activities of drawing and coloring. Each two-page spread has a scene for you and your child to create together, by drawing and coloring to complete the scene. The artist Chad Geran has thoughtfully left parts of each scene blank so you and your child can draw them in together, each taking a side. A prompt is included with each scene to help direct you, but feel free to draw and color wherever you want. There are no limits when it comes to creativity! Here are a few things to note:

⬦ Both left-handed and right-handed children (and dads!) can enjoy the drawing and coloring templates.

⬦ Let your child draw or color whatever side they want! This is about spending time together and creating something you can cherish together.

⬦ You might notice we made this book a little bit wider than the average child's activity book so coloring and drawing "side by side" are a little easier!

There are six sections to this activity book that generally focus on the main areas of a child's development: self-perception, relationships, home life, school life, play, and imagination. All of the coloring and drawing scenes in each section are designed to open up a dialogue about that part of your child's world. In the beginning of each section, you will find a brief description about typical childhood development in the area, along with a list of questions to help get a conversation started with your child. You can prompt your child using the suggested conversation starters I provided, the artwork on the page, or come up with your own creative questions! Don't forget: let your child lead the discussion, even if it's not what you thought you'd be talking about. This is about seeing your child's world and connecting with him or her in an authentic way.

QUALITY TIME COUNTS!

Try to set aside a period of uninterrupted time for you and your child to create together. You might have an hour or you might have 15 minutes. The length of time is not as important as the quality of the time you have together. So shut off the TV, put your phone on silent, and choose a quiet space to spread out and create! Here are a few things you can communicate to your child before you get started:

◇ Talk about basic expectations for Draw and Color Time with your child. This is especially important if you are limited on time. Let your child know how long you have to color/draw together to avoid a meltdown or disappointment if you have to stop before your child is naturally ready.

◇ Draw and Color Time is a special time for the two of you to create and talk together. It is important your child knows that he or she can say and share anything during this time.

◇ It is equally important for your child to know that it is alright if he or she does not want to talk. Don't worry. As you have more quality time together and practice the child-centered techniques below, eventually even a reluctant talker will start to open up.

HOW TO USE CHILD-CENTERED TECHNIQUES TO CONNECT

Your child has to follow a myriad of rules over the course of the day—at home, at daycare, at school, at dance class, or at sports practice. They constantly have to balance their inner desires—which is usually "I just want to play"—with the demands of the environment they are in. In fact, there are very few opportunities for children to take the lead in their daily lives.

In the therapeutic setting, I use what is called a **child-centered approach**, which is defined by play therapy guru Garry Landreth as following a child's lead and "looking through the child's eyes to understand the child's perception of self and experiences." It is essentially a nonjudgmental and nondirective way of interacting with your child. It means engaging in the activity from a place of observation, curiosity, and a willingness to learn about your child, rather than trying to teach, guide, or change your child. This might be difficult for some parents because we are so used to providing guidance to our children. Using child-centered techniques during your Draw and Color Time will set this time apart from the rest of your child's busy (adult-centered!) day. Fifteen minutes a day of focused child-centered interaction can do wonders for your child's sense of security, emotional growth, cognitive development, and self-esteem. Yes, quality time counts!

THE DOS AND DON'TS OF CHILD-CENTERED TIME

⬦ **Observe and describe** your child's creative process throughout your Draw and Color Time together. Here are some examples of descriptive phrases:

"YOU PICKED YELLOW FOR THE SUN."

"YOU'RE DRAWING A HAPPY FACE ON THE ELEPHANT."

"LOOK AT ALL THE DIFFERENT SHADES OF RED YOU ARE USING."

"LOOKS LIKE YOU'RE THINKING ABOUT WHAT TO DRAW NEXT."

Taking the time to narrate and describe your child's actions communicates that you are tuned in, paying attention, and happy to be spending time with him or her.

⬦ **Reflect your child's feelings.** You may notice that your child seems happy while drawing with you or frustrated when he or she cannot make it look quite right. Use these opportunities to reflect and validate your child. Here are some ways to reflect feelings:

"YOU ARE CALM AND HAPPY WHEN WE DRAW TOGETHER."

"YOU CAN'T FIND THE YELLOW CRAYON. THAT IS SO FRUSTRATING."

"YOU'RE PROUD OF WHAT YOU'RE MAKING."

"YOU'RE UPSET BECAUSE IT DIDN'T TURN OUT THE WAY YOU WANTED."

Reflecting your child's feelings also increases your child's sense that you ultimately understand his or her unique experience. This form of caring interaction will increase feelings of love and security and allow your child to open up more spontaneously.

⬦ **Avoid placing demands** on your child during Draw and Color Time. Commands such as "Sit over here" and "Give me that crayon" actually take the lead away from your child, according to the 2010 book *Parent-Child Interaction Therapy* by Cheryl McNeil and Tony Hembree-Kigin. This could potentially lead to tension if your child ignores or disobeys the command. The purpose of this quality time is to tune in to your child's world and it is difficult for your child to let you in when he or she is focused on obeying commands.

✧ **Avoid directing or criticizing your child's creative process.** It is important to refrain from any comments that change your child's creative process or criticize his or her choices. Even a well-intentioned, playful comment such as "The sun isn't purple, silly" can communicate to your child, "You're wrong." Also, avoid pointing out any mistakes you think your child made, such as drawing the wrong expression on a character or coloring outside of the lines. What may seem like a mistake to you could actually be your child experimenting with creative expression. The 2010 book by McNeil and Hembree-Kigin found that commenting on the "mistake" could have the unintended consequence of making your child feel bad and introduce some unpleasantness into your interactions during a time that should be enjoyable for both of you.

HOW TO USE SPECIFIC PRAISE TO INCREASE CONNECTION

Throughout Draw and Color Time, you might find yourself wanting to tell your child "Good job!" While this often-used phrase feels good in the moment to a child, it is very general and does not let your child know what he or she is doing well. According to McNeil and Hembree-Kigin's 2010 book, specific praise is a powerful tool to not only increase your child's self-esteem, but also improve or prevent negative behavior. Here are some examples of specific praise:

"IT'S NICE TO SIT AND DRAW CALMLY WITH YOU."

"YOU LIKE TO COLOR OUTSIDE THE LINES. YOU'RE SO CREATIVE."

"YOU'RE REALLY PAYING ATTENTION WHILE WE DRAW TOGETHER."

"I LOVE ALL THE COLORS YOU ARE USING."

"GOOD JOB DRAWING ALL THOSE LITTLE DETAILS."

HOW TO START A CONVERSATION WITH YOUR CHILD... AND KEEP IT GOING!

Once your child is settled into Draw and Color Time, and hopefully, in a peaceful state, you can begin to open up a conversation to learn more about his or her inner world. Start by asking **open-ended questions**, which require more detailed responses than "yes" or "no." Make sure your questions are **specific and focused** on a topic. A question like

"How was your day?" is very general, and it could be why your child answers with "fine," "good," "I don't know," or shrugged shoulders. Here are some examples of open-ended and specific questions about your child's day:

"TELL ME WHAT GAMES YOU PLAYED DURING RECESS TODAY."

"WHAT DID YOU LEARN TODAY IN SCIENCE?"

"TELL ME ABOUT CIRCLE TIME. WHAT SONGS DID YOU SING?"

"WHAT WAS YOUR DANCE TEACHER LIKE TODAY?"

Once your child gives you a response to a question, you can use **reflection and paraphrasing** to keep the conversation going, in addition to **follow-up questions**. Here is an example:

"WOW! YOU PLAYED HIDE-AND-SEEK WITH YOUR FRIENDS **[PARAPHRASE]**. THAT MUST HAVE BEEN SO MUCH FUN **[REFLECTION]**."

Pause and wait for your child to respond. If he or she answers with a simple "Yeah, I had fun," ask a follow-up question like "What was hard about the game?" or "What was it like when it was your turn to seek?" Keep going with this formula until the topic seems finished, at which point you can ask another open-ended question about a different topic. If your child changes the subject, go with him or her and continue to ask curious, open-ended, and specific questions.

If your child does not answer, he or she may not be ready to talk. Try a reflection phrase like "Hmm, I guess you don't want to talk about that," and then wait a few minutes and try another topic (or one you know your child likes to talk about). Remember, it is okay if your child does not openly share at first. By continuing to use the observation, description, and reflection techniques, he or she will eventually open up. It might take several Draw and Color Times. Be patient and trust that your child is appreciating the time you are taking to be present and connect.

WHAT SHOULD I DO IF...

... MY CHILD SHARES A VERY UPSETTING EXPERIENCE?

If your child brings up an experience from the day that is upsetting to hear, avoid going into advice-giving or problem-solving mode. In my work with families, I have seen parents enter advice-giving mode too quickly, and it frequently leads to the child getting frustrated or refusing to talk further. Draw and Color Time should be about learning about your child, not solving his or her problems. In a child-centered approach, you trust your child's inner drive to engage in healthy interactions with the world. Instead of giving advice, reflect feelings first (e.g., "I can see why that would upset you" or "That made you really mad"). Then try asking the following questions:

"WHAT DO YOU WISH WERE DIFFERENT?"

"WHAT WOULD YOU CHANGE ABOUT _____ ?"

"TELL ME YOUR IDEAS ABOUT WHAT YOU WILL DO/HOW YOU MIGHT HANDLE THIS."

. . . MY CHILD MISBEHAVES?

You might be wondering, "How can I be nondirective if my child starts to misbehave during Draw and Color Time?" Though the purpose of child-directed time is to allow your child freedom of expression in terms of thoughts, feelings, and desires, this does not mean that poor behavior is allowed. There will be times when your child pushes the limits (and your buttons)! Here are some ways to set limits based on the techniques advocated by Garry Landreth:

1   Acknowledge your child's feelings, wishes, and desires:

"I KNOW HOW MUCH YOU ENJOY DRAWING AND WANT TO DRAW EVERYWHERE."

2   Set the limit clearly and concisely:

"THE WALL/TABLE IS NOT FOR DRAWING."

3   Communicate appropriate alternative choices:

"YOU CAN DRAW IN THE BOOK WITH ME OR ON ANOTHER PIECE OF PAPER."

Additionally, I recommend communicating a consequence if your child ignores your set limit. "I really want to color with you, but if you choose to color on the wall again, we will stop." If you do set up a consequence, then you must be prepared to stop and clean up. Consistency here is essential. If your child protests, you still must stop Draw and Color Time, but you can say, "We'll try again tomorrow." Draw and Color Time is meant to be fun and positive, so if your child misbehaves there is no need for punishment. Stopping the activity is consequence enough.

. . . MY CHILD IS EASILY DISTRACTED OR UNFOCUSED?

A little preparation goes a long way for a child who is easily distracted. Take some time to minimize distractions before sitting down to draw and color. This includes turning the TV off, putting cell phones on silent, and minimizing other potential noises that typically distract your child.

Also be mindful of your child's age and what he or she is capable of in terms of maintaining attention. A general guide you can use is 3 to 5 minutes per year. So a 3-year-old's typical attention span is 9 to 15 minutes, while a 6-year-old can focus for 18 to 30 minutes. If your child can only do 5 or 10 minutes of Draw and Color Time that is completely okay! Remember, this time is about quality not quantity, and you want your child to feel positive about the experience when it is over. As time goes on, you may find your child's ability to focus is enhanced by coloring/drawing together.

During Draw and Color Time, you can also offer specific praise when your child is able to focus. For example, you can point out how he or she is concentrating or how calm his or her body is while drawing and coloring.

. . . MY CHILD IS A PERFECTIONIST?

You know you have a perfectionist child if he or she wants to get things just right and will spend a long time making this happen. He or she gets frustrated when things do not turn out the way it was envisioned (or compared to yours) and might even make comments like "This isn't good." Your instinct might be to tell your child, "It's okay. It doesn't have to be perfect." Even though your intentions are to support your child, this statement can actually send your child the message that something is wrong with him or her because from his or her point of view it does have to be perfect! For whatever reason, your child has an intrinsic tendency toward perfectionism, and it is very important to him or her. It likely causes anxiety when he or she is told it's okay when everything in his or her body says it is not. Use the reflection techniques during Draw and Color Time to validate your child's internal experience and communicate that you accept this part of him or her, rather than trying to correct it. Here are some validating statements:

"YOU ARE TRYING SO HARD TO GET IT JUST RIGHT."

"YOU'RE SO FRUSTRATED BECAUSE IT DOESN'T LOOK THE WAY YOU WANT."

"IT GOT MESSED UP! I CAN UNDERSTAND WHY THAT WOULD UPSET YOU."

After validating your child's feelings, you can model some ways to handle the internal frustration, such as engaging in positive self-talk: "Oh, I wanted to draw this just right and I keep messing it up. I'm frustrated with myself, but I like how this part turned out." Or, "I'm okay with this mistake because I really like drawing and coloring."

. . . MY CHILD IS NOT INTERESTED IN DRAWING OR COLORING?

Even with all your great intentions of trying to connect with your child through Draw and Color Time, you may have a child who is just not interested. Perhaps he or she does not enjoy drawing or coloring or would rather be doing something else. Since the goal of Draw and Color Time is to be child-centered and help your child share thoughts and feelings, it is important to honor when your child does not want to color or draw. You can say something like "I really want to spend some special time with you. If you don't want to draw or color that's okay. Would you rather _____?" Give your child some choices of other art activities, such as painting, finger-painting, drawing, molding clay or Play-Doh, or crafting with paper, stickers, or other materials. You can use the same child-centered play techniques, specific praise, and conversation starters during any of these activities, so don't feel pressured to stick only with drawing and coloring.

HAPPY COLORING!

— JASMINE NARAYAN, PSY.D.

SELF-PERCEPTION
"HOW I FEEL ABOUT MYSELF"

Children are in a constant state of growth, both emotionally and physically, with each day often bringing new tasks or skills to master. With each new stage of growth, your child develops self-worth, which includes thoughts and feelings about who he or she is and what he or she can do. Young children between the ages of 2 and 3 tend to define themselves based on concrete characteristics, abilities, and possessions, such as "I am a boy," "I can run," and "I have a train." As children mature, their sense of selves expand to include complex traits, such as "I love to ride my bike," "I am a good friend," and "I'm not as fast at running as my friends." The drawing and coloring scenes in this section, coupled with the conversation starters below, are designed to give you a window into the inner workings of your child's mind, and more importantly, his or her budding sense of self.

LET'S TALK ABOUT IT!

Remember, this is a child-centered activity, so let your child lead the way. Here are some additional conversation starters that you can use for any of the drawing templates in this section if you wish.

- WHAT DO YOU LOVE ABOUT YOURSELF?
- WHAT WOULD YOU CHANGE ABOUT YOURSELF? (TO BE MORE SPECIFIC, FOR A YOUNGER CHILD, YOU CAN ASK WHAT HE OR SHE LIKES/DISLIKES ABOUT HIS OR HER APPEARANCE OR PERSONALITY.)
- WHAT MAKES YOU SMILE? LAUGH? HAPPY?
- WHAT MAKES YOU ANGRY? SAD?
- WHAT ARE YOU AFRAID OF?
- WHAT MAKES YOU FEEL BETTER WHEN YOU ARE ANGRY? SAD? SCARED?
- TELL ME ABOUT YOUR FAVORITE ACTIVITY? HOBBY? SPORT?
- WHAT KINDS OF THINGS ARE YOU GOOD AT DOING?
- TELL ME ABOUT SOMETHING THAT IS HARD FOR YOU TO DO.
- WHAT/HOW DO YOU WANT TO BE WHEN YOU GROW UP?
- WHAT DO YOU LIKE/DISLIKE ABOUT BEING A KID?
- WHAT SONG/COLOR/MOVIE DO YOU LOVE MOST?

WHAT DO YOU WANT TO BE WHEN YOU GROW UP?
DRAW IT IN!

START THE CONVERSATION!

RELATIONSHIPS
"HOW I FEEL ABOUT MY FAMILY AND FRIENDS"

The drawing and coloring scenes in this section depict family relationships and other important connections for your child, such as playing with friends and peers. For young children, the world centers around them and their immediate families. It is with these early connections that children first learn how to love and be loved. As they mature, children take these ways of relating and apply them to outside interactions. The suggested conversation starters below are meant to open a dialogue about how your child perceives his or her most important relationships and can provide information on how to increase your positive connection with each other.

LET'S TALK ABOUT IT!

Remember, since this is a child-centered activity, let your child lead the way. Here are some additional conversation starters that you can use for any of the drawing templates in this section if you wish.

- ✦ WHAT IS YOUR FAVORITE THING TO DO WITH _____ (MOM/DAD/BROTHER/SISTER/GRANDMA/GRANDPA)?

- ✦ WHAT MAKES A GOOD FRIEND? TELL ME HOW YOU ARE A GOOD FRIEND.

- ✦ WHEN YOU ARE SAD/ANGRY/SCARED, WHAT CAN I DO TO MAKE YOU FEEL BETTER?

- ✦ TELL ME A STORY ABOUT _____ (PICK A PERSON IN THE CHILD'S LIFE).

- ✦ WHAT DO LOVE ABOUT YOUR BEST FRIEND? WHAT DO YOU DISLIKE ABOUT YOUR BEST FRIEND?

- ✦ WHAT DO YOU LIKE TO DO WITH YOUR BEST FRIEND?

- ✦ WHAT IS AWESOME/HARD ABOUT PLAYING ON A TEAM?

- ✦ HOW DO YOU SHOW SOMEONE YOU LOVE THEM?

- ✦ HOW DO YOU KNOW I LOVE YOU?

- ✦ WHAT WOULD YOU LIKE US TO DO MORE OF TOGETHER?

- ✦ WHO IS THE KINDEST/MEANEST PERSON YOU KNOW?

- ✦ WHO DO YOU WANT TO BE LIKE WHEN YOU GROW UP?

- ✦ IF YOU COULD CHANGE SOMETHING ABOUT OUR FAMILY, WHAT WOULD YOU CHANGE?

HOME LIFE
"HOW I SEE MY HOME"

The drawing and coloring scenes in this section reflect the many aspects of your child's home life, including common routines, such as getting ready for school, self-care, mealtime, and bedtime. While children of all ages need structure and rules to increase their sense of safety and trust in the world, their thoughts and feelings about those routines and rules may vary. The suggested conversation starters below are meant for you to learn more about your child's perspective on family life, rules, and expectations at home, as well as to allow room for your child to express the full range of his or her opinions.

LET'S TALK ABOUT IT!

Remember, this is a child-centered activity, so let your child lead the way. Here are some additional conversation starters that you can use for any of the drawing templates in this section if you wish.

- ✧ WHAT IS YOUR FAVORITE TIME OF DAY? SEASON? HOLIDAY?
- ✧ WHAT DO YOU LIKE/DISLIKE ABOUT OUR HOME?
- ✧ WHAT WOULD YOU CHANGE ABOUT WHERE WE LIVE?
- ✧ WHAT RULE IS THE HARDEST TO FOLLOW IN OUR HOME?
- ✧ WHAT RULES DO YOU THINK WE SHOULD HAVE FOR OUR FAMILY?
- ✧ IF YOU COULD PLAN OUR DINNER TOMORROW, WHAT WOULD YOU MAKE/WANT TO EAT?
- ✧ WHAT MAKES OUR FAMILY SPECIAL?
- ✧ WHAT IS YOUR FAVORITE PART OF _____ (INSERT FAMILY HOLIDAY TRADITION)?
- ✧ IF YOU COULD LIVE ANYWHERE IN THE WORLD, WHERE WOULD YOU WANT TO LIVE?

COLOR IN THIS
SPRINGTIME
SCENE!

SOME OF THE FLOWERS ARE MISSING IN THE GARDEN BELOW.
DRAW THEM IN!

COLOR IN THE **CARNIVAL** SCENE!

THE CLOWN SEEMS TO BE MISSING HIS SHOES.
DRAW THEM IN!

COLOR IN THE FAMILY ROOM!

IT'S FAMILY MOVIE NIGHT!
WHAT MOVIE IS THE FAMILY ENJOYING?
DRAW IT IN!

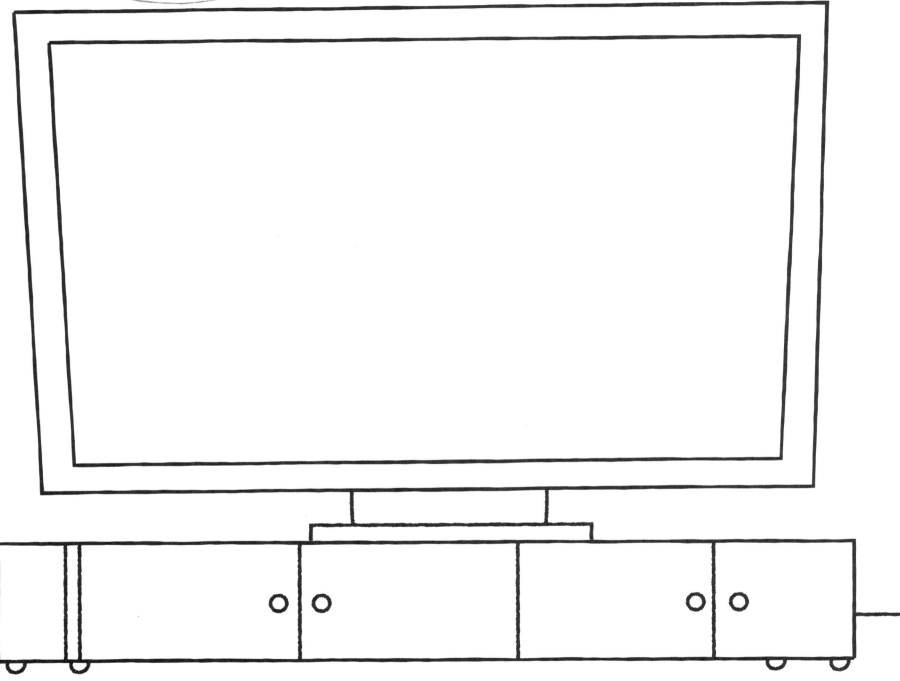

SCHOOL LIFE
"HOW I SPEND MY TIME AT SCHOOL"

The drawing and coloring scenes in this section represent your child's school and learning experiences. As children grow, they spend more time at school, where this environment becomes an important place to nurture self-esteem and independence. For some children, school is an exciting source of learning and fosters feelings of accomplishment, while other kids may struggle with learning and feel disappointed in themselves. The conversation starters below are designed to help you explore your child's feelings about school, as well as the aspects of the learning environment where your child feels more or less confident so that you can provide support.

LET'S TALK ABOUT IT!

Remember, this is a child-centered activity, so let your child lead the way. Here are some additional conversation starters that you can use for any of the drawing templates in this section if you wish.

- ✧ WHAT DO YOU LIKE/DISLIKE ABOUT SCHOOL?
- ✧ WHAT'S YOUR FAVORITE SUBJECT IN SCHOOL?
- ✧ WHAT SUBJECT DO YOU HAVE TO WORK HARD AT IN SCHOOL?
- ✧ WHAT DO YOU LIKE/DISLIKE ABOUT YOUR TEACHER? WHAT DOES HE/SHE LOOK LIKE/SOUND LIKE?
- ✧ WHO DO YOU SIT NEXT TO IN CLASS? WHAT DO YOU THINK ABOUT HIM OR HER?
- ✧ WHAT DID YOU LEARN TODAY IN MATH/SCIENCE/CIRCLE TIME/GYM?
- ✧ TELL ME SOMETHING YOU DID AT RECESS TODAY?
- ✧ HOW DO YOU FEEL WHEN YOU ARE IN CLASS? ON THE PLAYGROUND? IN THE CAFETERIA?
- ✧ IF YOU COULD CHANGE ONE RULE IN YOUR CLASSROOM, WHAT WOULD IT BE?
- ✧ WHAT IS THE FUNNIEST THING THAT HAPPENED AT SCHOOL TODAY?
- ✧ IF YOU COULD BE THE TEACHER, WHAT WOULD YOU TEACH YOUR CLASSMATES?

HOW DO YOU FEEL WHEN SPEAKING IN
FRONT OF YOUR CLASSMATES?

START THE
CONVERSATION!

COLOR IN THE LIBRARY SCENE!

ADD MORE WONDERFUL THINGS COMING OUT OF THE BOOK.
DRAW THEM IN!

START THE CONVERSATION!

WHAT IS YOUR FAVORITE THING TO READ ABOUT?

WHAT IS YOUR FAVORITE SONG?

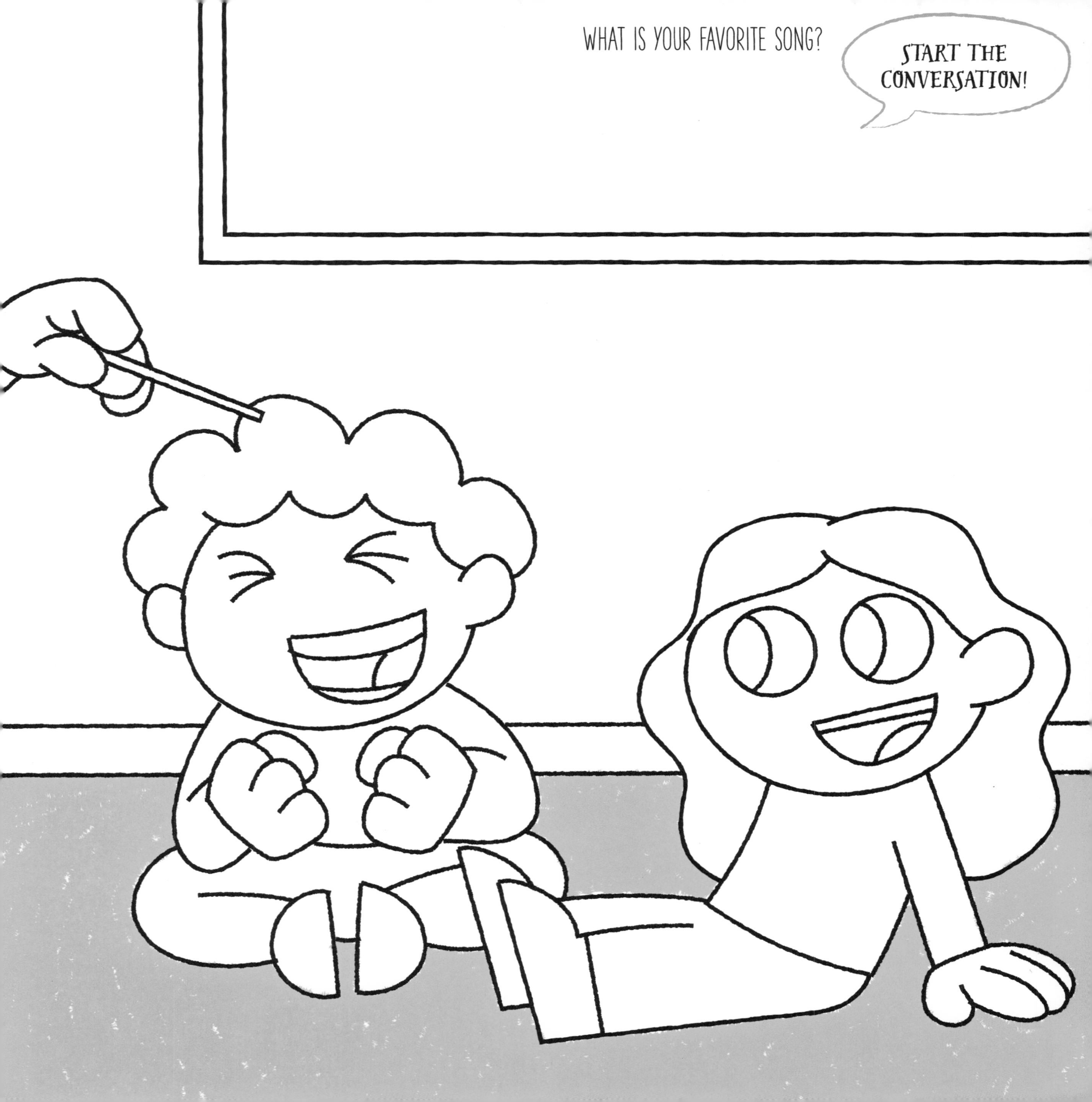

COLOR IN THIS LUNCHTIME SCENE!

THE BOY WALKING BY LOOKS LIKE HE COULD USE A SEAT TO EAT HIS LUNCH.
DRAW IN A PLATE AT THE TABLE FOR HIM.

WHAT WOULD YOU DO IF SOMEONE WAS SITTING ALONE AT LUNCH?

START THE CONVERSATION!

IMAGINATION
"GET TO KNOW MY CREATIVE SIDE"

The drawing and coloring scenes in this section are meant to tap into your child's silly, whimsical, and imaginative nature, a crucial aspect of childhood. Young children tend to have "magical" thinking, which fuses elements of reality with ideas that defy logic and adult sensibility. Even in a child's wildest fantasies, there are grains of truth and hints of unexpressed desires. The conversation starters below are designed to help you find those grains hidden in your child's fantastical imaginings.

LET'S TALK ABOUT IT!

Remember, this is a child-centered activity, so let your child lead the way. Here are some additional conversation starters that you can use for any of the drawing templates in this section if you wish.

- ✧ WHAT DOES YOUR IMAGINARY FRIEND LOOK LIKE?
- ✧ IF YOU HAD A MILLION DOLLARS, WHAT WOULD YOU BUY?
- ✧ IF YOU COULD MAKE UP A WEIRD PET, WHAT WOULD IT BE?
- ✧ WHAT KINDS OF THINGS DO YOU THINK ARE IN THE SKY, BEYOND THE STARS AND THE MOON?
- ✧ WHERE WOULD YOU WANT TO GO ON AN ADVENTURE?
- ✧ IF I HAD A MAGIC WAND AND COULD GRANT YOU THREE WISHES, WHAT WOULD YOU WISH FOR?
- ✧ WHAT DO YOU BELIEVE IN, EVEN THOUGH SOMEONE TOLD YOU IT IS NOT REAL?

COLOR IN THE OUTER SPACE SCENE!
WHAT DO YOU THINK IS ON THE MOON?
DRAW IT IN!

WHERE WOULD YOU WANT TO GO IN SPACE?

START THE CONVERSATION!

COLOR IN THE SPOOKY SCENE!

WHAT DO YOU THINK THE WITCHES ARE COOKING IN THAT POT? DRAW IT IN!

WHAT CREATURES DO YOU THINK
MIGHT LIVE IN OUTER SPACE?

START THE
CONVERSATION!

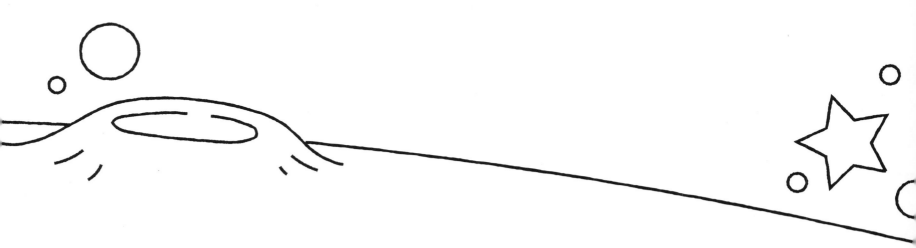

WHAT AMAZING ANIMAL DOES THE GIRL SEE IN THE JUNGLE?
DRAW IT IN!

IF YOU COULD DEVELOP A POTION TO CURE ANYTHING IN THE WORLD, WHAT WOULD YOU CURE?

START THE CONVERSATION!

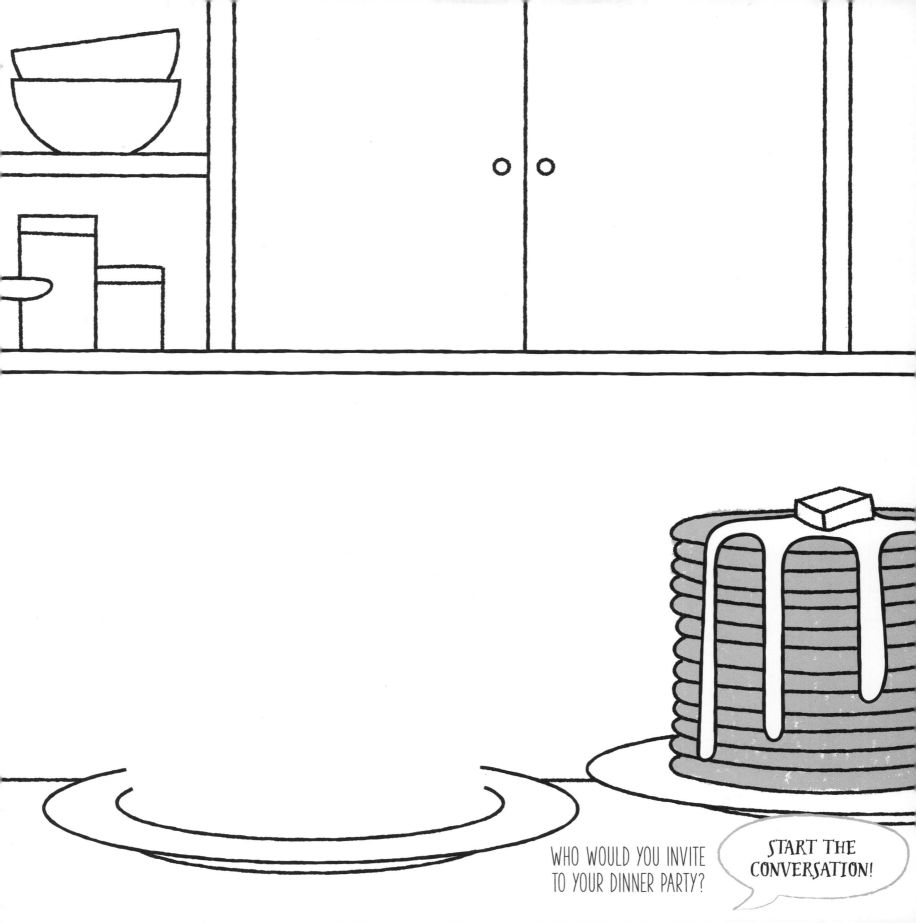

PLAY
"HOW I LIKE TO HAVE FUN AND EXPRESS MYSELF"

Sure, it looks like all fun and games on the surface, but on a deeper level, play is one of the most important building blocks of childhood. In fact, in 1989, the United Nations identified play as a fundamental right and an activity that is essential for optimal development. Why? Simply put, play is when children express feelings and needs that they cannot easily talk about, as well as practice new skills, socialize, and try out social or gender roles. The conversation starters below will help you tap into your child's innate playful and creative spirit.

LET'S TALK ABOUT IT!

Remember, this is a child-centered activity, so let your child lead the way. Here are a few conversation starters that you can use for any of the drawing templates in this section if you wish.

- ✧ TELL ME ABOUT YOUR FAVORITE GAME/WHAT YOU LIKE TO PLAY WITH? WHAT DO YOU LOVE ABOUT THAT GAME/TOY?
- ✧ WHAT DO YOU LIKE TO PLAY BY YOURSELF? WITH OTHERS?
- ✧ TELL ME SOMETHING YOU PLAYED AT SCHOOL TODAY? AT DAYCARE? AT RECESS?
- ✧ WHAT DO YOU LIKE TO PRETEND TO DO? WHO DO YOU PRETEND TO BE WHEN YOU ARE PLAYING?
- ✧ IF YOU INVITED YOUR FAVORITE CARTOON CHARACTER OVER FOR A PLAYDATE, WHAT WOULD HAPPEN?
- ✧ WHO DO YOU HAVE THE MOST FUN WITH?
- ✧ WHO DO YOU WISH YOU HAD MORE TIME TO PLAY WITH?
- ✧ WHAT GAME/SPORT/ACTIVITY DO YOU ENJOY DOING EVEN IF YOU'RE NOT SO GREAT AT IT?

COLOR IN THE **BEACH** SCENE!

A FISH HAS JUST JUMPED OUT OF THE WATER TO SAY HELLO. **DRAW IT IN!**

WHAT DO YOU ENJOY DOING AT THE BEACH?

START THE CONVERSATION!

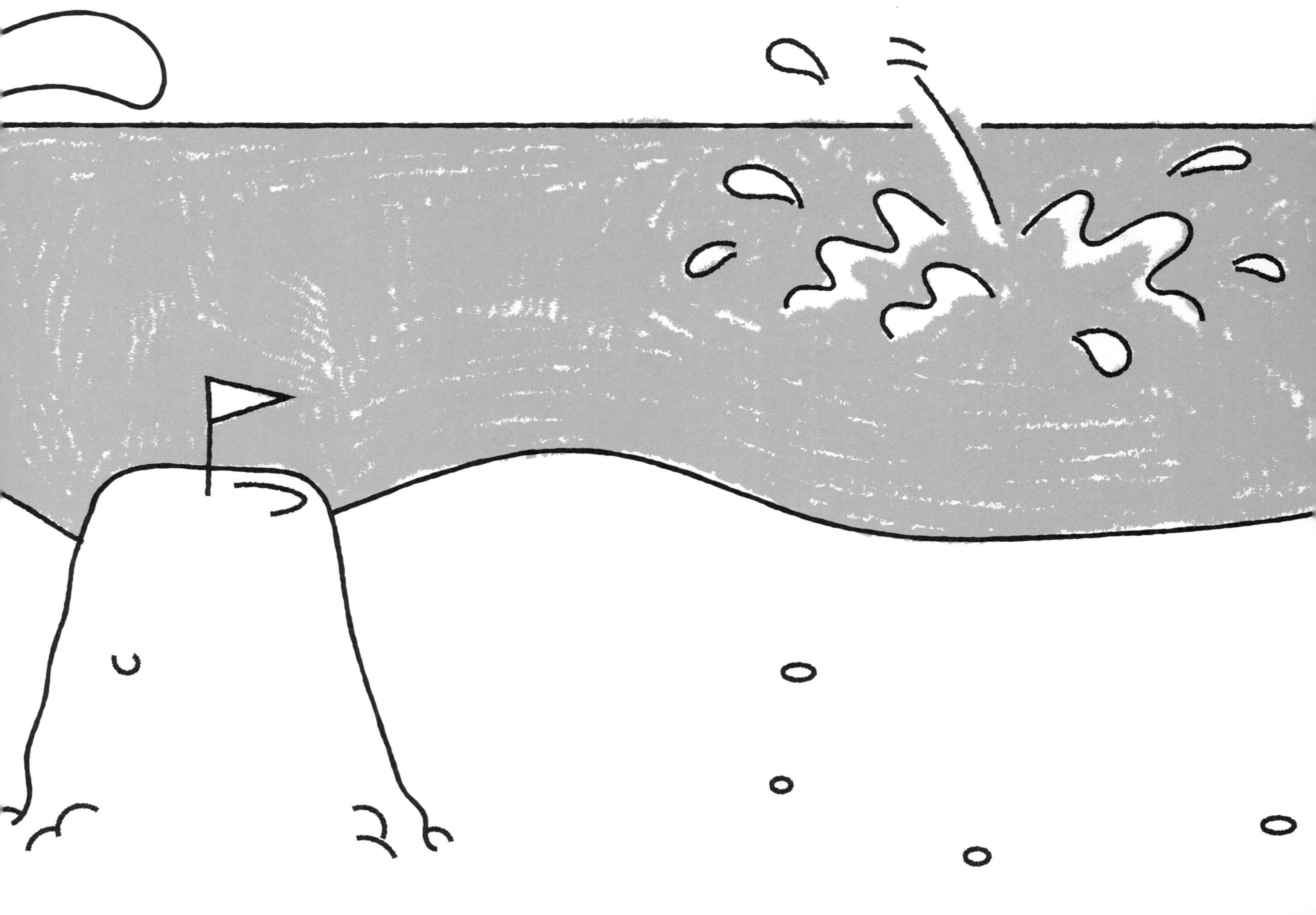

COLOR IN THE PUPPET THEATER!

WHAT KIND OF PUPPET SHOW IS BEING PUT ON? DRAW IN THE MISSING SCENERY!

WHAT KIND OF SHOWS DO YOU LIKE TO PREFORM FOR YOUR FAMILY?

START THE CONVERSATION!

COLOR IN THE **WESTERN** SCENE!

WHAT IS THIS COWGIRL TRYING TO CATCH WITH HER LASSO? **DRAW IT IN!**

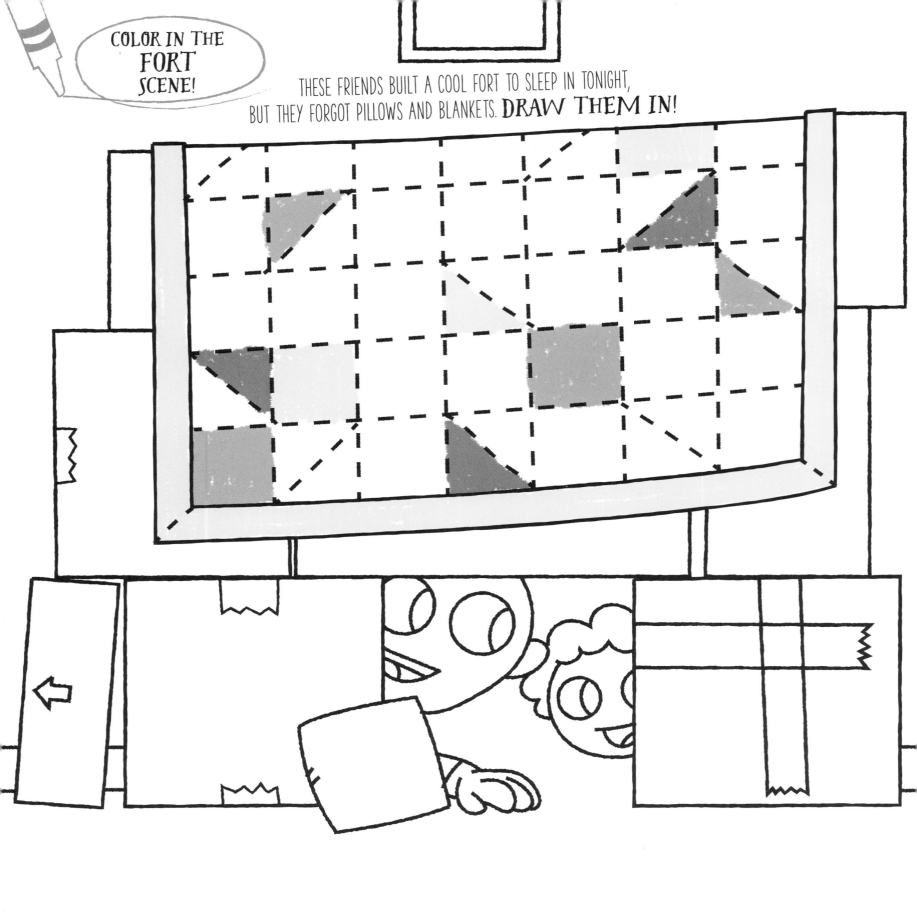

REFERENCES

Birch, J. and K. Carmichael. "Using Drawings in Play Therapy: A Jungian Approach," *The Alabama Counseling Association Journal* 34:2 (2009): 2–7.

Homeyer, L.E. and M.O. Morrison. "Play Therapy: Practice, Issues and Trends," *American Journal of Play* 4 (2008): 210–228.

Landreth, G. *Play Therapy: The Art of the Relationship* (3rd ed.). New York: Routledge, 2012.

McNeil, C.B. and T.L. Hembree-Kigin. *Parent-Child Interaction Therapy (Issues in Clinical Psychology)* (2nd ed.). New York: Springer, 2010.

ABOUT THE AUTHOR

Jasmine Narayan, Psy.D., is a Licensed Clinical Psychologist who attained her doctorate from the University of Hartford, where she received specialized training in child and adolescent psychology.

Dr. Narayan is dedicated to empowering children and teens who struggle with emotional regulation, aggressive/impulsive behavior, ADHD, depression, anxiety, and trauma. She also works closely with families, drawing on positive parenting techniques and behavioral interventions to increase positive connections and healthy communication between parents and children.

As a huge proponent of the creative arts and an avid Zentangler, Dr. Narayan incorporates art and coloring in her therapeutic work as well. She is co-founder of Family Guiding Psychological Services, PLLC, an organization based in Huntington, New York, that effectively serves individuals and families from diverse backgrounds through psychotherapy, consultation, and online resources.

You can learn more about Dr. Narayan and read her articles at www.familyguiding.com or you can follow her on Twitter @DrJNarayan.

ABOUT THE ILLUSTRATOR

Chad Geran lives in Regina, Canada, with his wife and two sons. He is the fourth best drawer in his house. Visit him online at geran.ca.